Fault Lines Participants' Guide

fault lines

Participants' Guide

The Social Justice
Movement and
Evangelicalism's
Looming
Catastrophe

Voddie T. Baucham Jr.

SALEM
BOOKS
an imprint of Regnery Publishing

All Scriptures are taken from THE HOLY BIBLE, ENGLISH STANDARD VERSION.® Copyright © 2001 by Crossway, a publishing ministry of Good News Publishers. Used by permission. All rights reserved.

Salem Books™ is a trademark of Salem Communications Holding Corporation. Regnery® and its colophon are registered trademarks of Salem Communications Holding Corporation.
Cataloging-in-Publication data on file with the Library of Congress.

ISBN: 978-1-68451-459-5
DVD Edition ISBN: 978-1-68451-502-8

Published in the United States by
Salem Books
An Imprint of Regnery Publishing
A Division of Salem Media Group
Washington, D.C.
www.SalemBooks.com

Manufactured in the United States of America

10 9 8 7 6 5 4 3 2 1

Books are available in quantity for promotional or premium use. For information on discounts and terms, please visit our website: www.SalemBooks.com.

Contents

A Word from Voddie

Welcome to the *Fault Lines Participants' Guide*! I'm so glad you're here.

This is an important time in history. We are in the midst of a spiritual battle as "woke" and morally bankrupt doctrines infiltrate our schools, our families, and our churches.

I liken this current moment to two people standing on either side of a major fault line just before it shifts. When the shift comes, the ground will open up, a divide that was once invisible will become visible, and the two will find themselves on opposite sides of it. That is what is happening in our day. Churches are splitting. Denominations are in turmoil. Relationships are severed. And I don't believe the fracture in this fault line is yet even a fraction of what it will be.

Make no mistake. We live in a fallen world replete with real problems like hatred, injustice, oppression, and racism, to name a few. These are not narratives or figments of our imaginations. They are real and they exist. In fact, they remind us that we are broken and that we need reconciliation to a God who saves through Jesus Christ. This is the Gospel, the Good News, the answer to all of humanity's failures and frailties. At least it used to be. But somehow today for many, even for well-meaning people who claim to follow Jesus, it doesn't seem to be enough.

I believe the current concept of social justice is incompatible with biblical Christianity. In fact, we are beginning to see a new hermeneutic develop from the movement of cultural social justice. Specifically, sin is viewed as institutional as opposed to being in the heart of man. Social justice has become a religion in which the answer for oppression and inequity is found in something other than the forgiveness we find through God in Christ.

There are plenty of sincere, though perhaps naïve, Christians who, if they knew the ideology behind the term "social justice," would run away from it like rats from a burning ship. These two words sound great. Who wouldn't want to be about the business of social justice, right? Yet without biblical and theological literacy, we won't understand the full meaning of the term, and we will unknowingly miscommunicate and undermine the message of the Gospel.

As followers of Jesus Christ, our responsibility is to follow Truth. There can be no reconciliation without justice. That is absolutely true! And the death of Christ is that justice. I believe in racial reconciliation. I must, because I believe the Bible.

My aim in this guide is to offer you an opportunity to learn and reflect on how and why the current movement to enact social justice is in direct opposition to biblical justice. I want to help you think biblically, not create opinions based on your feelings or spout certain rhetoric because you're backed into a corner. I want to show you how you can find freedom from this ideology and forgiveness through the sacrifice of Jesus Christ alone.

Let's get started!

Voddie Baucham

How to Use This Guide

If you are working through this guide in a group setting, great! If not, you can also use it on your own. The questions offered can be used either way. I highly recommend watching the video segments in conjunction with this teaching. Finally, you'll have a more meaningful and insightful experience with this guide if you read it in conjunction with my book *Fault Lines*, which I'll be referring to at times. If you choose to use this guide on its own, don't worry—you'll still gain plenty of value.

This guide is divided into six sessions that each include:

1. *Big Idea* (a one-line overview of the session)
2. *Looking Back* (Sessions 2–6; a brief look in the rearview mirror at the previous session)
3. *Primer* (an introduction to the session)
4. *Talk about It* (an icebreaker question to set the tone)
5. *Video Session Notes* (an outline of highlights from the video segment, plus room for notetaking)
6. *Discussion* (questions based on the Bible, the book, and the video to initiate conversation and provoke thought)
7. *Wrap-Up and Closing Prayer* (a brief summation of the session and a prayer to end the session)

8. *Between Sessions* (two days of Scripture study and reflection questions to deepen your understanding)

What You'll Need:

Unless otherwise marked, all the Scripture references in this guide are from the English Standard Version Bible (ESV). If you prefer a different translation, feel free to use it or a Bible app to look up the verses. Space is provided for you to jot down notes, answer questions, or write anything you wish.

Social Justice: What It Really Means

Big Idea

Understanding the difference between social justice and biblical justice is essential to correctly communicating the Gospel of Christianity. Social justice is concerned with groups of people and has to do with the state redistributing resources to achieve equal outcomes. Biblical justice is centered on the law of God and deals primarily with the heart.

Primer

As you can imagine, I have often been accused of not having empathy or compassion for minorities who have been the victims of racism. It's rather preposterous considering my background.

I was born in 1969 and was raised by a single mother in the drug-infested, gang-ridden city of Los Angeles. For the longest time, Malcolm X was my greatest hero. Throughout the years, I've been pulled over by cops for no legitimate reason. In fact, one time, while walking with a friend, we found ourselves lying facedown on the sidewalk while police officers questioned us. When I made the decision to leave a predominantly black church for a predominantly white church, my family and I were on the receiving end of statements that ranged from insensitive to downright racist. So yes, of course I understand the sting of racism.

In the same vein, I also understand that we are all sinners. The cops who pulled me over for what might have been the amount of melanin in my skin and the people who made racist remarks toward our family weren't taking their cues from a script designed to keep me down. They were sinners. Like me. Like you.

There came a time in my life when I realized my identity was steeped more in my race as a black man than who I was in Jesus Christ. As human beings we have the tendency to define who we are not just by our race, but by our ethnicity, our zip code, our parent's legacy, any number of things. Who we are, however, is grounded in Whose we are. The Gospel is not something that merely sits on top of our identity. When we come to Christ, our identity is transformed completely. As Paul tells us,

> From now on, therefore, we regard no one according to the flesh. Even though we once regarded Christ according to the flesh, we regard him thus no longer. Therefore, if anyone is in Christ, he is a new creation. The old has passed away; behold, the new has come. (2 Corinthians 5:16–17)

When you become a new creation in Christ, justice, among other things, is not an option, it's a command. But it's not about following whatever social justice trend is attracting the most attention; it's learning the right meaning of the word "justice" as the Bible describes it and enacting it appropriately. And before we do that, it's critical to understand the meaning of certain words we're hearing when it comes to social justice vernacular.

 Talk about It

How have you fought injustice in your church/school/community?

WATCH THE VIDEO

 Video Teaching Notes

Watch Video Session 1. Use the outline and space below to jot down notes or record key ideas.

- The Gospel will always be the Gospel. However, we are not always faithful in the way that we communicate the Gospel.

- Micah 6:8: "What does the Lord require of you but to do justice, and to love kindness, and to walk humbly with your God?"

- Justice is not optional for the people of God.

- Justice means the righteous and impartial application of the law of God in a given circumstance.

- Note: Below are definitions and assumptions of critical social justice derived from a worldview alien to the Bible. Definitions are summarized by Voddie Baucham, unless otherwise noted:

  - **Social justice:** "Justice at the level of society or state as regards the possession of wealth, commodities, opportunities, and privileges." In other words, social justice is "distributive justice."[1]

  - **Equity:** everyone is guaranteed the same outcome.

- **Racial justice:** the systemic fair treatment of people of all races, resulting in equitable opportunities and outcomes for all.

- **Whiteness:** a set of normative privileges granted to white-skinned individuals and groups, which is invisible to those privileged by it.

- **White privilege:** a series of unearned advantages that accrue to white people by virtue of their whiteness.

- **White supremacy:** any belief, behavior, or system that supports, promotes, or enhances white privilege.

- **White equilibrium:** a cocoon of racial comfort, centrality, superiority, entitlement, racial apathy, and obliviousness, all rooted in an identity of being good people free of racism.

- **White fragility:** the inability and unwillingness of white people to talk about race due to the grip that whiteness, white supremacy, white privilege, white complicity, and white equilibrium exert on them, either knowingly or unknowingly.

💬 Discussion

1. How did you define social justice before watching the video or reading the book? What informed your definition of this term?

2. In the video teaching, Voddie defines biblical justice as "the righteous and impartial application of the word of God." How does this shape your definition of social justice in the previous question?

3. Are there forms of social justice that are antithetical to what God says in the Bible?

4. What is one practical way to enact biblical justice, or, as Voddie defines it, "to apply God's Law equally across the board"?

5. Have you ever been wronged and sought revenge or justice as a result? What was the outcome? What did you learn from that experience?

6. What does the Bible mean to you? How often do you search the Scriptures to find answers to common social problems or challenges?

7. In *Fault Lines*, Voddie writes:

> Beyond confronting falsehoods in general, our pursuit of justice must also be characterized by a

pursuit of truth. Much has been said recently about seeking justice, and I could not agree more. However, we must be certain that we pursue justice on God's terms.

Name an instance where you have pursued justice on God's terms.

8. What is one example of the difference between equity and equality?

 ## Wrap-Up and Closing Prayer

Today we learned the differences between social justice and biblical justice and how important it is to define words correctly before subscribing to an ideology that may oppose our faith.

You can pray the following prayer to close this session or say one your way:

God, thank You for Calvary's love. Grant by Your grace that I may never become jaded or get used to the magnitude of Your love and its implications in my life. Teach me, correct me, rebuke me, train me, and conform me to the image of Your beloved Son. In other words, let Your Word have its way in my life. In Christ's name I pray, amen.

Between Sessions

DAY 1

Read Micah 6:8:

> "He has told you, O man, what is good;
>   and what does the Lord require of you
> but to do justice, and to love kindness,
>   and to walk humbly with your God?"

In two to three sentences, summarize the main ideas of the above passage.

One of my main objectives in this study is for you to understand the difference between social justice and biblical justice, then put biblical justice into practice. Review the differences in the below table:

Social Justice	Biblical Justice
Affects a group of people	Affects individuals/ the heart
Concerns state/ federal laws	Concerns the law of God
Has to do with equity and outcomes	Has to do with equality and opportunities
Injustice defined as anything that produces or allows an inequitable outcome	Injustice defined as anything that fails to rise to the level of the law of God

In your own words, describe the differences between "social justice" and "biblical justice."

Read the Parable of the Talents Jesus told in Matthew 25:14–30:

[14] For it will be like a man going on a journey, who called his servants and entrusted to them his property. [15] To one he gave five talents, to another two, to another one, to each according to his ability. Then he went away. [16] He who had received the five talents went at once and traded with them, and he made five talents more. [17] So also he who had the two talents made two talents more. [18] But he who had received the one talent went and dug in the ground and hid his master's money. [19] Now after a long time the master of those servants came and settled accounts with them. [20] And he who had received the five talents came forward, bringing five talents more, saying, "Master, you delivered to me five talents; here, I have made five talents more." [21] His master said to him, "Well done, good and faithful servant. You have been faithful over a little; I will set you over much. Enter into the joy of your master." [22] And he also who had the two talents came forward, saying, "Master, you delivered to me two talents; here, I have made two talents more." [23] His master said to him, "Well done, good and faithful servant. You have been faithful over a little; I will set you over much. Enter into the joy of your master." [24] He also who had received the one talent came forward, saying, "Master, I knew you to be a hard man, reaping where you did not sow, and gathering where you scattered no seed, [25] so I was afraid, and I went and hid your talent in the ground.

Here, you have what is yours." [26] But his master answered him, "You wicked and slothful servant! You knew that I reap where I have not sown and gather where I scattered no seed? [27] Then you ought to have invested my money with the bankers, and at my coming I should have received what was my own with interest. [28] So take the talent from him and give it to him who has the ten talents. [29] For to everyone who has will more be given, and he will have an abundance. But from the one who has not, even what he has will be taken away. [30] And cast the worthless servant into the outer darkness. In that place there will be weeping and gnashing of teeth."

In this parable, we see the master distributing different amounts of money to each of the three servants. Some followers in the social justice movement would say this was a discriminatory, unjust act. In alignment with this type of ideology, we would see the one servant with the most talents redistributing them so each servant would have an equal amount. But this is not what happens. In the parable the master gave each servant a specific number of talents "according to his ability" (v. 15). This tells me some of the servants had more business or financial acumen than the others. When the master came back and checked on the progress of the investments, the unprofitable servant's talent was taken away from him and given to the one who made the most with his investment.

Was each servant given an equal opportunity? Why or why not?

Does every individual share the same talents, skills, and abilities? Does this mean that we are all not equal?

If you have more (wealth/power/authority/access/resources) than others, how should you act? What if you have less?

Considering what you've learned in this session, list three ways you can "do justice" in your family/workplace/community according to Micah 6:8.

Meditate and Memorize: Micah 6:8 (translation of your choice)

DAY 2

It is the Bible—not sociology, psychology, or political science—that offers sufficient answers not only on race, but on every ethical issue man has faced or will ever face.

When we talk about the term "biblical justice," it's important to remind ourselves of the authority, sufficiency, and inerrancy of the Bible.

The Bible is made up of sixty-six different books written on three continents (Asia, Africa, and Europe) in three languages (Greek, Hebrew, and Aramaic) by more than forty authors over a period of about fifteen hundred years. Findings at well over twenty-five thousand archeological digs have confirmed the accuracy of historical events recorded in the Bible.[2] There's a lot of concrete evidence to substantiate the veracity of the Scriptures other than our experiences or the fact that we were raised in church and that's just what we believe.

I choose to believe the Bible because it's a reliable collection of historical documents, written by eyewitnesses during the lifetime of other eyewitnesses, that reports supernatural events that took place in fulfillment of specific prophecies, and the authors claim their writings are divine rather than human in origin.

The Bible is the Word of God. Christians need to be firm in their belief that the Word of God is truth. God spoke it to His people, and it is completely trustworthy.

Read the following Bible verses:

2 Timothy 3:16: "All Scripture is breathed out by God and profitable for teaching, for reproof, for correction, and for training in righteousness."

Romans 15:4: "For whatever was written in former days was written for our instruction, that through endurance and through the encouragement of the Scriptures we might have hope."

Acts 24:14: "But this I confess to you, that according to the Way, which they call a sect, I worship the God of our fathers, believing everything laid down by the Law and written in the Prophets."

Psalm 19:7–11: "The law of the Lord is perfect, reviving the soul; the testimony of the Lord is sure, making wise the simple; the precepts of the Lord are right, rejoicing the heart; the commandment of the Lord is pure, enlightening the eyes; the fear of the Lord is clean, enduring forever; the rules of the Lord are true, and righteous altogether. More to be desired are they than gold, even much fine gold; sweeter also than honey and drippings of the honeycomb. Moreover, by them is your servant warned; in keeping them there is great reward."

2 Peter 1:20–21: "Knowing this first of all, that no prophecy of Scripture comes from someone's own interpretation. For no prophecy was ever produced

by the will of man, but men spoke from God as
they were carried along by the Holy Spirit."

Do you believe the Bible tells the absolute truth? Why or why not?

How often do you turn to the Bible to define terms, gain wisdom,
or seek clarity on challenging situations?

How has the Bible informed your faith?

Why can you believe the Bible?

How do you need to change your Bible study habits in light of the
importance of Scripture? Write down three actions steps to make
it happen—then do them!

It's Not What You Think: A Look at Cultural Narrative

Big Idea

Real justice requires truth, not a false narrative.

Looking Back

Share one thing that stood out to you most from last week's lesson, video, reading, or discussions.

Primer

Today, people are rioting, making assumptions, and demanding justice before knowing the facts of a particular matter. No doubt social injustice is an emotional topic. Yet through the different narratives being pushed through social media and the news, many people tend to reject objectivity in favor of believing a story told only from one side—a story that can not only obscure but lie about the true facts of what really happened.

In my book *Fault Lines*, I explore the consequences of false narratives in depth and cite many different examples in which I dismantle the myths being pushed, including the story that white cops are hunting down and killing unarmed black men. In the limited space I have in this guide, I'll offer one example from my extensive research in this regard.

You have probably heard the popular statistic that underlies this narrative: that police are two and a half times more likely to shoot and kill a black man than a white man. This ratio supposedly proves systemic racism. But does it really?

A National Academy of Sciences study ignited controversy when its authors proclaimed, "We find no evidence of anti-Black or anti-Hispanic disparities across shootings, and White officers are not more likely to shoot minority civilians than non-White officers."[3]

In fact, if we apply the same logic across the board, we find systemic injustice in police shootings based on sex, age, geographic region, population, and a host of other factors. Let's take gender into consideration. According to a database maintained by the *Washington Post*, 95 percent of the 7,349 people killed by police since 2015 were men.[4] If we use the same logic employed by those who claim the black/white shooting stats prove racial bias, wouldn't we have to conclude that the overwhelming disparity in the male/female stats proves misandry? Of course, no one is making this claim. Why? Because in this case we readily admit that a univariate analysis is inadequate to explain the disparity. We also know that males commit most violent crimes,[5] which is the top predictor of violent interactions with police.

Without careful and thoughtful pause, we allow false narratives to continue to propagate and further create division and strife in our country, our churches, and our communities. I certainly don't deny that racism and racial disparities exist in the United States, but I also don't believe it is a systemic problem that lies in the DNA of this country.

We must love our God, His Gospel, and our sisters and brothers enough to challenge false narratives. However, in doing so, we need to go deeper. We need to apply the truth of Scripture found in Proverbs 18:13 and 17:

> If one gives an answer before he hears, it is his folly and shame. . . . The one who states his case first seems right, until the other comes and examines him.

Only by addressing and seeking out the truth will we be able to push back the lies and walk in true reconciliation.

💬 Talk about It

Have you ever believed a narrative from a headline, a social media post, or a video clip without examining or researching the full story?

WATCH THE VIDEO

 Video Teaching Notes

Watch Video Session 2. Use the outline and space below to jot down notes or record key ideas.

- Story of Tony Timpa

- One of the most significant issues we face is the underlying narrative that we use to interpret events. Whether, how, and when we respond is often determined by our assumptions.

- "If one gives an answer before he hears, it is his folly and shame" (Proverbs 18:13).

- "The one who states his case first seems right, until the other comes and examines him" (Proverbs 18:17).

Discussion

1. Was there a time you knowingly or unknowingly told or spread a lie? What was the outcome? In hindsight, what should you have done instead?

2. Before watching the video teaching, had you ever heard of Tony Timpa and the manner of his death?

3. In *Fault Lines*, Voddie says that according to the religion of the social justice movement, "narrative is an alternative and ultimately superior truth." Give an example from the video teaching or real life of how a narrative was ultimately determined to be false. What was the outcome?

4. Read Proverbs 6:16–19:

> There are six things that the LORD hates, seven that are an abomination to him: haughty eyes, a

lying tongue, and hands that shed innocent blood,
a heart that devises wicked plans, feet that make
haste to run to evil, a false witness who breathes out
lies, and one who sows discord among brothers.

How do you see the things that God hates in this Scripture evidenced in the current social justice movement?

5. What are some current social justice narratives that you need to do a better job of investigating, detonating, or keeping from propagating?

6. On which do you place more weight, the Bible or someone's personal experience? How can we appreciate and respect a person's story while enacting the truth of the Gospel?

7. What is an internal false narrative you have believed that has proven destructive to your faith or relationship with God? Do you still believe it? Why or why not?

8. Have you ever been the victim of a false narrative? What happened?

⊘ Wrap-Up and Closing Prayer

Today we learned about false narratives and the importance of listening with discernment and paying attention to the full picture of a situation, rather than just one side.

You can pray the following prayer to close this session, or say one your way:

> God, open my heart and my mind to seek and find Truth. May I not be so blinded in my thoughts or feelings that I cannot discern what is true. Clothe me with the wisdom I need to make the right decisions. Remind me to seek Your truth in Your Word rather than in my story or the narratives of others. In Christ's name I pray, amen.

Between Sessions

DAY 1

When evaluating people's testimonies and pleas, it's important to bear in mind the words of John 7:51: "Does our law judge a man without first giving him a hearing and learning what he does?" It is also important to remember two specific passages in the book of Proverbs that we will focus on in this last segment.

Today, we're going to look at Proverbs 18:17. Read the following Scripture: "The one who states his case first seems right, until the other comes and examines him."

Paraphrase the main idea of the above verse in your own words.

Write down a real-life example of this Scripture in practice.

Recall an instance when you have not practiced the wisdom of this truth. What was the outcome? What should you have done instead?

If we're honest, most of us would admit we talk more than we listen. In the same vein, most of us fall prey to the seductive lure of shallow yet emotional soundbites, video clips, or headlines we see instead of thinking first. Rather than forming opinions, commenting, or giving answers before we know the full story, we must learn not only to listen, but to listen with discernment.

Read Hebrews 5:14: "But solid food is for the mature, for those who have their powers of discernment trained by constant practice to distinguish good from evil."

How do you define the word "discernment"?

I've often heard Christians speak of this as if it were a kind of gift, a special ability to look at something or someone and see what lies beyond. This is false. In fact, what I've just described is mysticism. Discernment is not something you fall out of bed and acquire; it's something you develop through discipline.

When you encounter a tense or sensitive situation in which you're trying to figure out what is right and true, how do you put your discernment skills to the test?

I like what John MacArthur said about discernment. "In its simplest definition, discernment is nothing more than the ability to decide between truth and error, right and wrong. Discernment is the process of making careful distinctions in our thinking about truth. In other words, the ability to think with discernment is synonymous with an ability to think biblically."[6]

Here are four steps you can take, starting now, to begin to sharpen your discernment tools:

1. Read the Bible.
2. Think biblically.
3. Pray biblically.
4. When in doubt, repeat #1–3.

Meditate and Memorize: Proverbs 18:13 (translation of your choice)

DAY 2

Read Proverbs 18:17: "The one who states his case first seems right, until the other comes and examines him."

Paraphrase the main idea of the above verse in your own words.

Write down a real-life example of this Scripture in practice.

If you're a parent of small kids, you've probably had the honor of at least once walking into a room and finding a ball lying next to a previously unbroken object, and two kids who say the same thing: "I didn't do it. He/she did." Well, who do you believe? And how do you go about finding out the truth?

This process is like our legal judicial system, which of course is a lot more complex than questioning two toddlers about a shattered vase they both deny breaking. You hear the accounts of all parties. You gather and study the evidence. You elicit the testimonies of eyewitnesses. You do all these things before pointing an accusatory finger at the individual you *think* or *feel* was in the wrong.

God does not need a second opinion.

- He sees everything. (Proverbs 15:3: "The eyes of the Lord are in every place, keeping watch on the evil and the good. He knows everything.")

- He knows everything. (1 John 3:20: "For whenever our heart condemns us, God is greater than our heart, and he knows everything.")

We are not God, however, and unlike Him, we can get stuck in a narrow position. But when we seek to understand the different sides to every story and garner more information in the process, we can form wiser and more informed opinions.

Read Proverbs 18:2: "A fool takes no pleasure in understanding, but only in expressing his opinion."

Why don't fools need more information/evidence to thoroughly assess a situation?

Meditate and Memorize: Proverbs 18:17 (translation of your choice)

Critical Race Theory: A Wolf in Sheep's Clothing

Big Idea

Critical Race Theory (CRT) stems from an analytical tool that challenged traditional legal scholarship and embraces central tenets that oppose the idea of the sufficiency of Scripture.

Looking Back

Share one thing that stood out to you most from last week's lesson, video, reading, or discussions.

Primer

My book *Fault Lines* dives deeply into the origins and intricacies of CRT, yet you can observe the anti-Christian thread from the following condensed version.

Critical Theory was established as a philosophical and analytical tool in the 1930s. Through the writings of American legal scholars such as Richard Delgado, Kimberlé Crenshaw, and Derrick Bell, CRT morphed into a worldview that is antithetical to what the Bible teaches. Below are the four main tenets of CRT:

- Racism as normative (it's normal, it's everywhere, and it's unavoidable)

- Interest convergence (white people are unable to take righteous action against racism unless it converges with their own individual interests)

- Anti-objectivity

- The social construction of knowledge

CRT teaches that the *only* way to understand racism and oppression is to elevate black voices over others'. Those who disagree with that narrative are either racist or suffer from internalized racism. However, we do not need CRT to teach us about race or the sin of partiality; we have the sufficiency of Scripture for that.

Philosophies like CRT appeal to Christians because we are rightly concerned with fighting injustices such as racism. Some Christians may not be totally sold on this ideology, but cherry-pick elements of CRT that they agree with. However, this works about as well as cherry-picking which elements of Buddhism you would celebrate as a Christian.

In short, Critical Race Theory is at odds with Christianity because it takes the problem of racism out of the individual heart and into social systems and structures.

💬 Talk about It

If applicable, share your personal experience or knowledge regarding CRT outside of what you've learned from this study guide, video teaching, or the book *Fault Lines*.

WATCH THE VIDEO

🎬 Video Teaching Notes

Watch Video Session 3. Use the outline and space below to jot down notes or record key ideas.

- Tenets of CRT according to Richard Delgado, one of its founders

  1. "Racism is ordinary, not aberrational—'normal science,' the usual way society does business,

the common, everyday experience of most people of color in this country."[7]

2. "Because racism advances the interests of both white elites (materially) and working-class people (psychically), large segments of society have little incentive to eradicate it."[8]

3. "The 'social construction' thesis holds that race and races are products of social thought and relations. Not objective, inherent, or fixed, they correspond to no biological or genetic reality; rather, races are categories that society invents, manipulates, or retires when convenient."[9]

4. "The notion of a unique voice of color . . . the voice-of-color thesis holds that because of their different histories and experiences with oppression, black, Indian, Asian, and Latino/a writers and thinkers may be able to communicate to their white counterparts matters that the whites are unlikely to know."[10]

- CRT is not just an analytical tool but a clear ideology in direct opposition to the truth of the Word of God.

- From a biblical perspective, no individual or group of individuals can be written off because of what their ancestors did. According to CRT, white people are inherently guilty of racism by virtue of their whiteness. They are also irredeemable.

- While CRT argues that knowledge is socially constructed, Christianity teaches there is objective truth and that we access it through the general and special revelation of God.

🗨 Discussion

1. Before reading this study and watching the video, how would you describe your understanding of CRT?

2. Share your experience with the teachings of CRT, whether in a professional setting or in your child's school curriculum.

3. In *Fault Lines*, Voddie defines CRT as follows:

> CRT recognizes that racism is engrained in the fabric and system of the American society. The individual racist need not exist to note that institutional racism is pervasive in the dominant culture. This is the analytical lens that CRT uses in examining existing power structures. CRT identifies that these power structures are based on white privilege and white supremacy, which perpetuates the marginalization of people of color.[11]

How does the above definition as well as the video teaching reshape your answer to the previous question?

4. Do you consider yourself a racist or antiracist? Why or why not?

5. Read Matthew 15:19–20: "For out of the heart come evil thoughts, murder, adultery, sexual immorality, theft, false witness, slander. These are what defile a person." What does the Bible say about the source of sin?

6. Read Genesis 1:26–27: "Then God said, 'Let us make man in our image, after our likeness.' . . . So God created man in his own image, in the image of God he created him; male and female he

created them." Who did God make in His image? How can we treat everyone as image-bearers of God?

7. How does CRT shame groups of people? How does this contradict the way in which God deals with our repentant sin? (See Romans 8:1: "There is therefore now no condemnation for those who are in Christ Jesus.")

8. Is the root of evil in sin, or in systems?

⊘ Wrap-Up and Closing Prayer

Today we highlighted the faulty worldview of CRT and how it compares to the message of redemption recorded in the Bible.

You can pray the following prayer to close this session, or say one your way:

> God, be the light on my path as I thirst for Your truth. Cultivate in me a loyalty that is not divided between You and the world. Strengthen my pursuit of wisdom and knowledge as I seek to discern what is right and what is not. In Christ's name I pray, amen.

Between Sessions

DAY 1

We're going to biblically tackle the four tenets of CRT in this week's Between Sessions. Today, we will focus on the first two:

- Racism as normative (it's normal, it's everywhere, and it's unavoidable)

- Interest convergence (white people are unable to take righteous action against racism)

CRT views the world through the lenses of power dynamics and racial oppression. White people are born as oppressors into a system designed to benefit only the members of their own group. Minorities, on the other hand, are born into this world oppressed, disadvantaged, and marginalized. This is simply the way it is, whether or not we recognize it.

Read the following Bible verses:

1 Corinthians 15:49: "Just as we have borne the image of the man of dust, we shall also bear the image of the man of heaven."

Romans 5:12: "Therefore, just as sin came into the world through one man, and death through sin, and so death spread to all men because all sinned . . ."

Romans 6:11: "So you also must consider yourselves dead to sin and alive to God in Christ Jesus."

Everyone on this earth is born with the same condition: sin. It is only when we are alive in God through Christ Jesus that we become new creatures. In accordance with the Scripture above, how does our sinful condition put us all on equal footing before God?

Read Deuteronomy 16:19–20:

You shall not pervert justice. You shall not show partiality, and you shall not accept a bribe, for a bribe blinds the eyes of the wise and subverts the cause of the righteous. Justice, and only justice, you shall follow, that you may live and inherit the land that the Lord your God is giving you.

The Bible acknowledges oppression but does not label certain ethnicities as oppressors.

While CRT argues that racism is inherent in our culture, our systems, and our identities, the Bible teaches that human beings have a systemic sin problem. Racism is just one of its many symptoms.

What are some other symptoms of the systemic sin problem?

How does CRT promote division rather than reconciliation?

As Christians, we do not pursue equal outcomes, but righteous application of God's law. Read Romans 13:8-10:

> Owe no one anything, except to love each other, for the one who loves another has fulfilled the law. For the commandments, "You shall not commit adultery, You shall not murder, You shall not steal, You shall not covet," and any other commandment, are summed up in this word: "You

shall love your neighbor as yourself." Love does no wrong to a neighbor; therefore love is the fulfilling of the law.

We have an opportunity to say to a world seeking the false, inadequate, burdensome law of antiracism, "We have something better; something more." How can we walk in reconciliation? Through forced legislation or turning our hearts over to Jesus?

DAY 2

Today we're going to dive into the last two tenets of CRT:

- Anti-objectivity
- The social construction of knowledge

A biblical worldview starts with the knowledge of the one true and living God. "In the beginning, God created the heavens and the earth" (Genesis 1:1).

Read the following Bible verses:

John 14:6: "Jesus said to him, 'I am the way, and the truth, and the life. No one comes to the Father except through me.'"

Psalm 119:160: "The sum of your word is truth, and every one of your righteous rules endures forever."

John 17:17: "Sanctify them in the truth; your word is truth."

James 1:17: "Every good gift and every perfect gift is from above, coming down from the Father of lights, with whom there is no variation or shadow due to change."

What do these verses say about God and truth?

According to CRT, there is no such thing as objective truth, as knowledge is socially constructed. In this worldview, only minorities, or the oppressed, have unique access to the truth through their stories of oppression. The idea that there is special knowledge or revelation available to some and hidden from others by virtue of their race or position in the oppressor/oppressed scheme is unthinkable—and unbiblical.

Read the following Bible verses. How does God's Word contradict CRT?

Ephesians 2:18: "For through him we both have access in one Spirit to the Father."

Ephesians 2:14: "For He Himself is our peace, who made both groups into one and broke down the barrier of the dividing wall."

Romans 2:11: "For God shows no partiality."

Galatians 3:28: "There is neither Jew nor Greek, there is neither slave nor free, there is no male and female, for you are all one in Christ Jesus."

Critical Race Theory will not have the last word. God's Church will neither fall nor fail. It is "a pillar and buttress of the truth" (1 Timothy 3:15), and God's Word "is firmly fixed in the heavens" (Psalm 119:89). We can hold on to hope because we know that "the grass withers, the flower fades, but the word of our God will stand forever" (Isaiah 40:8). I know God will save His people and vindicate His name. I also know that He will do it through Christians who heed the call to "remember the Lord, who is great and awesome, and fight for your brothers, your sons, your daughters, your wives, and your homes" (Nehemiah 4:14).

What is one way you and your family can fight to help defeat CRT, this wolf in sheep's clothing?

SESSION 4

One Size Does Not Fit All: Disparities Do Not Equal Discrimination

Big Idea

According to CRT, disparities among different groups of people, specifically whites and minorities, are *de facto* evidence of racism. The only solution is to redistribute power and resources so each group has the same amount.

Looking Back

Share one thing that stood out to you most from last week's lesson, video, reading, or discussions.

Primer

CRT and the thought leaders who evangelize its core messages hold that systemic racism is the cause of disparities between certain groups of people. For example, the reason a high percentage of black men (versus white men) are in prison, black families (versus white families) live in impoverished communities, blacks (versus whites) lack a college education or even a high school degree is because of 1) the color of their skin and 2) the system they were born into was constructed to keep them down. Yet the reality is that systemic racism isn't always the reason for these problems.

Just as the maxim I learned in my college statistics class, "Correlation does not equal causation," says, there are legitimate explanations other than racism for troubling problems in minority communities. I offer a slew of them in my book. The current social justice movement, however, rejects these explanations; no other options beyond systemic racism are to be considered. In fact, doing so would label you as a racist who wants to protect your power and keep those disparities in place. This has to be true because if you were not racist, you would know that the cause of disparities is...racism.

Yet the major underlying malady that contributes to these and other social ills is immorality and fatherlessness. We know that fatherlessness is the number one indicator of future violence, dropouts, out-of-wedlock births, and incarceration. And in the black community, more than 70 percent of all children are born out of wedlock![12] Even Barack Obama mentioned this in a speech he gave on Father's Day in 2008 at the Apostolic Church of God in Chicago.[13]

It is overly simplistic to say that disparities equal discrimination. I believe there is racism. I believe there are racists. However, I reject the idea that America is "characterized by racism," or that racism is an unavoidable byproduct of our national DNA. In fact, America is one of the least racist multiethnic countries in the world.

We can't paint in broad strokes. If we see racist or unjust actions, we must address them. But to automatically assign guilt to a group of people is injustice.

💬 Talk about It

What disparities do you observe between different groups of people in your community?

WATCH THE VIDEO

🎞 Video Teaching Notes

Watch Video Session 4. Use the outline and space below to jot down notes or record key ideas.

- The term "racial injustice" stems from a presupposition that disparities are evidence of injustice.

- Illustration of distributing milk crates so each person can watch the baseball game.

- From a biblical perspective, we know there are disparities and that disparities aren't always wicked. (See Parable of the Talents.)

- This is a narrative that assumes the only way one person can have an advantage is that they somehow oppressed others in order to get it.

- If you attribute disparities to anything other than racism, you are participating in aversive racism.

- We've moved into territory that represents arguments and opinions that are raised against the knowledge of God.

Discussion

1. Do you see all disparities between blacks and whites as the result of systemic racism? Why or why not?

2. Whose responsibility is it to address disparities in a given community?

3. In *Fault Lines*, Voddie writes, "Any attempt to explain the disparity as anything other than racism is, according to DiAngelo, another form of racism called 'aversive racism.'" Is the term "aversive racism" biblical? Why or why not?

4. What do we call taking resources/money/access from someone who has them and giving them to someone who does not for the sole reason that they do not?

5. How can behavioral inequalities (like poor decisions) lead to financial, educational, or other inequalities?

6. Read Romans 3:9–18:

> What then? Are we Jews any better off? No, not at all. For we have already charged that all, both Jews and Greeks, are under sin, as it is written: "None is righteous, no, not one; no one understands; no one seeks for God. All have turned aside; together they have become worthless; no one does good, not even one." "Their throat is an open grave; they use their tongues to deceive." "The venom of asps is under their lips." "Their mouth is full of curses and bitterness." "Their feet are swift to shed blood; in their paths are ruin and misery, and the way of peace they have not known." "There is no fear of God before their eyes."

What does this Scripture say about the state of *all* people?

7. As Christians, why should we teach what we believe in the Bible versus the teachings of the current social justice movement, and specifically CRT?

Wrap-Up and Closing Prayer

Today we have learned that disparities do not equal discrimination. Pray the following prayer to close this session, or say one your way:

God, I thank You for the knowledge and wisdom You give and for the hope that is in me. I pray I am able to give an answer for that hope and share with others the truth of the Gospel. Give me a spirit that's teachable so I may be a living sacrifice for the sake of Your name. In Christ's name I pray, amen.

SESSION 4

Between Sessions

DAY 1

In a secular society that praises individualism, it seems odd that the social justice movement, which believes racism is inherent and inescapable among white people, sees them not as individuals, but as part of a certain group and therefore part of the problem.

The very idea of dividing people by ethnicity, then declaring some of them wicked oppressors and others the oppressed, is inconsistent with the biblical doctrine of universal guilt:

> What then? Are we Jews any better off? No, not at all. For we have already charged that all, both Jews and Greeks, are under sin, as it is written: "None is righteous, no, not one; no one understands; no one seeks for God. All have turned aside; together they have become worthless; no one does good, not even one." "Their throat is an open grave; they use their tongues to deceive." "The venom of asps is under their lips." "Their mouth is full of curses and bitterness." "Their

feet are swift to shed blood; in their paths are ruin and misery, and the way of peace they have not known." "There is no fear of God before their eyes." (Romans 3:9-18)

This is not the state of white men; it is the state of all men. How does God hold us responsible for the sins of our neighbor, a stranger across the country, a parent?

Read the following Scripture:

Jeremiah 1:5: "Before I formed you in the womb I knew you, and before you were born I consecrated you."

Psalm 139:13-16: "For you formed my inward parts; you knitted me together in my mother's womb. I praise you, for I am fearfully and wonderfully made. Wonderful are your works; my soul knows it very well. My frame was not hidden from you, when I was being made in secret, intricately woven in the depths of the earth. Your eyes saw my unformed substance; in your book were written, every one of them, the days that were formed for me, when as yet there was none of them."

Galatians 6:4: "But let each one test his own work, and then his reason to boast will be in himself alone and not in his neighbor."

1 Samuel 16:7: "For the Lord sees not as man sees: man looks on the outward appearance, but the Lord looks on the heart."

What do the above Bible verses tell us about how God sees each of us as individuals?

If God sees us as individuals, how are we accountable for the sins of our forefathers?

Read Romans 3:10: "None is righteous, no, not one."

No single group possesses all the good. Just like no single person has the key to a blameless life.

What does "righteous" mean? What are some characteristics of righteousness?

Can anyone keep God's law perfectly? Why or why not?

DAY 2

The preponderance of evidence shared by those promoting racial justice as the pressing need of the day is rooted in the assumption that every disparity is *de facto* evidence of racism.

Jemar Tisby, author of *The Color of Compromise*; Latasha Morrison, author of *Be the Bridge*; and Daniel Hill, author of *White Awake*, all tout the common refrain that the U.S. Constitution counted slaves as three-fifths of a white citizen. Thus, this "fact" is yet another piece of evidence to prove systemic racism. But is it true?

If you have heard of the "three-fifths compromise," where did you hear/read about it? What is your understanding of this agreement that has since been repealed?

Britannica sums up this legislative moment in history as follows:

> Having failed to secure the abolishment of slavery, some delegates from the Northern states sought to make representation dependent on the size of a state's free population. Southern delegates, on the other hand, threatened to abandon the convention if enslaved individuals were not

counted. Eventually, the framers agreed on a compromise that called for representation in the House of Representatives to be apportioned on the basis of a state's free population plus three-fifths of its enslaved population. This agreement came to be known as the three-fifths compromise.[14]

And straight from the Framers of the Constitution of the United States:

Representatives and direct Taxes shall be apportioned among the several States which may be included within this Union, according to their respective Numbers, which shall be determined by adding to the whole Number of free Persons, including those bound to Service for a term of years, and excluding Indians not taxed, three-fifths of all other Persons. (U.S. Constitution, Article 1, Section 2, Paragraph 3)

Can you write down/highlight/point out where in the above historical references, according to Jemar Tisby, that "instead of acknowledging the full humanity and citizenship of black slaves, political leaders determined that each slave would count as three-fifths of a white citizen"?[15]

If you stumbled on that last question, it was for good reason. Did you catch the phrase "three-fifths of all other persons" in the Constitution? There was no statement that slaves were three-fifths of a person. In fact, the statement affirms the personhood of those to whom it refers while allowing for only three-fifths of those "persons" to be included for the purpose of apportioning taxes and representatives. Anyone who says the U.S. Constitution calls slaves three-fifths human is ignorant at best. At worst, they are twisting historical facts in order to promote a critical social justice view of U.S. history.

What did you learn about this compromise that surprised you?

Read Galatians 3:26–29:

> For in Christ Jesus you are all sons of God, through faith. For as many of you as were baptized into Christ have put on Christ. There is neither Jew nor Greek, there is neither slave nor free, there is no male and female, for you are all one in Christ Jesus. And if you are Christ's, then you are Abraham's offspring, heirs according to promise.

How is equality among all people recognized by God and characteristic of the life of a believer?

SESSION 5

Uncovering Roots and a New Way to Interpret History

Big Idea

All ideas come from somewhere. Critical Theory, for instance, along with many pillars that undergird the current social justice movement, has its roots in Marxism. While we cannot excise an idea from its roots, we also cannot reframe history according to one limited lens—in this case, the lens of systemic racism.

Looking Back

Share one thing that stood out to you most from last week's lesson, video, reading, or discussions.

Primer

In order to understand the mission of social justice, you have to understand a couple of concepts, including CRT, which I've reviewed in Session 3, and Critical Theory. Critical Theory is CRT's predecessor.

German philosopher Karl Marx was the leading architect of the most dominant school of thought within sociology, known as Conflict Theory. Marx viewed society as different social classes all competing for a limited pool of resources such as food, housing, employment, education, and leisure time.[16] After the Marxist revolution failed to topple capitalism in the early twentieth century, many Marxists went back to the drawing board, modifying and adapting Marx's ideas. Antonio Gramsci, a neo-Marxist philosopher and a founding member of the Italian Communist Party, built on this ideology. In simple terms, in trying to figure out how the Marxist revolution failed and how it kept people from seeing how evil capitalism is, he developed the idea of hegemony: the concept of a ruling class in culture and society that establishes the rules of the game in order to benefit itself. This is a power struggle between oppressors and the oppressed. The idea took root in Frankfurt, Germany, through a group that came to be known as the Frankfurt School. These men developed Critical Theory as an expansion of Conflict Theory and applied it more broadly, including to other social sciences and philosophy. Their main goal was to address structural issues causing inequity.

In order to understand Critical Theory, it is important to understand how the words "critical" and "theory" are used. In the social sciences, "critical" is "geared toward identifying and exposing problems in order to facilitate revolutionary political change."[17] In other words, it implies revolution. It is not interested in reform. Hence, we do not "reform" the police; we "defund" or abolish them.

CRT's predecessor is not just an analytical tool, as some might argue; it is a worldview.

To partner with and even further this worldview, many social justice advocates are attempting to reframe the origin of America. The 1619 project, founded by *New York Times* Magazine reporter Nikole Hannah-Jones in August 2019, aims to move our understanding of the founding of America from 1776 to 1619, when the first enslaved Africans arrived in what would eventually become the Commonwealth of Virginia. Simply put, if we can rewrite history through that lens, then America is grounded in what activist Jim Wallace has called the original sin of slavery and racism.

All these things have nothing to do with the heart and everything to do with politics and power. This is antithetical to biblical justice in every way imaginable.

💬 Talk about It

When is reframing or retelling a story ever justified?

WATCH THE VIDEO

 Video Teaching Notes

Watch Video Session 5. Use the outline and space below to jot down notes or record key ideas.

- Ideas have consequences and origins.

- The Black Lives Matter movement has roots in Marxism.

- Karl Marx connects us to Antonio Gramsci and the idea of cultural hegemony, which leads us to the thought of the Frankfurt School and the ideology that says all relationships are based on power dynamics.

- The great debate between 1619 and 1776—changing America's birth year as 1619 reframes her as an oppressor.

- Are we what we say we are, or are we our worst moment?

- It is impossible to retell and restate all of history.

- Christians should retell history for the purpose of magnifying the God of history and His providence in dealing with men.

 Discussion

1. Our beliefs consist of ideas that influence our behavior and actions. Name one good and one bad idea from the last twenty years and discuss the results of each.

2. How does an ideology that supports the social structure of the have/have-nots and oppressor/oppressed tend to divide people rather than generate reconciliation?

3. How do you define "white privilege"? If you are white, name an unearned advantage you have that people of color do not. If you are a person of color, name something you were unable to accomplish/attain because of not having white skin.

4. Read Ezekiel 18. Does God hold us accountable for our parents' sins? Why or why not?

5. Read 2 Corinthians 10:5:

> We destroy arguments and every lofty opinion raised against the knowledge of God, and take every thought captive to obey Christ.

What does this Scripture teach us about believing and following false doctrine and ideas like the ones you are learning about in this session?

6. How does rewriting history promote personal accountability and responsibility in the present?

7. What role does history have in shaping the biblical view of social justice?

8. What are the consequences of reshaping America's past and reframing it as an oppressively racist nation, defined by its failures?

☑ Wrap-Up and Closing Prayer

In this section, we learned about the origin of CRT and Critical Theory and their relationship with the social justice movement. We also learned that this movement seeks to reframe the United States as a birthing place for hatred, racism, and discrimination by changing its founding date from 1776 to 1619. History is replete with good and bad, and can never be retold by every person and from every lens.

You can pray the following prayer to close this session, or say one your own way:

> God, we are at war with the world and in the Church, and we fight for what is true. May we not embrace ideologies that hold us hostage to emotional blackmail, but proclaim what You say in Your Word. Give me the strength and courage to refute destructive heresies and stand firm in the Gospel. In Christ's name I pray, amen.

Between Sessions

DAY 1

I believe we are being duped by an ideology bent on our demise. This ideology has used our guilt and shame over America's past, our love for our brethren, and our good and godly desire for reconciliation and justice as a means to introduce destructive heresies. We cannot embrace, modify, baptize, or Christianize these ideologies; we must identify, resist, and repudiate them.

Paul's admonishment to the Colossian church serves as a relevant warning to us today. Read Colossians 2:8–10:

See to it that no one takes you captive by philosophy and empty deceit, according to human tradition, according to the elemental spirits of the world, and not according to Christ. For in him the whole fullness of deity dwells bodily, and you have been filled in him, who is the head of all rule and authority.

Most scholars say that Paul was in prison in Rome when he wrote these words in a letter to the Colossian church in AD 60–61. While Paul had never visited the church in person, he loved the people, agonized in prayer for them, and was concerned about the dangerous teachings they were hearing. There were reports of false teachers denying the deity of Jesus. These teachers twisted the Gospel with popular Greek ideas to deny the saving power of Christ and belie the truth of the Good News.

No century, country, church, or community has been absent of deceptive ideologies that convincingly try to distort the truth. Think about the history of the church and the past ten years. What sorts of unbiblical doctrines have saturated the Christian world?

Have you ever been persuaded to believe these teachings? What was the outcome?

How does the current social justice movement use portions of biblical truth to enhance its arguments or reasoning?

Paul gives us great advice in Colossians 2:7 on how to walk in Jesus to stand firm in our faith:

> Therefore, as you received Christ Jesus the Lord, so walk in him, rooted and built up in him and established in the faith, just as you were taught, abounding in thanksgiving.

Notice the action phrases used in this Scripture:

- *Rooted* and *built* up in Him

- *Established* in the faith

- *Abounding* in thanksgiving

Write down five practical steps you can take, starting today, to walk in Him so you will not fall prey to false teaching.

DAY 2

In the video teaching, I highlight the 1619 Project and its goals. If we move the date America became a nation to 1619, we essentially declare that America is inherently and irreparably racist. In the video, I ask a pertinent question: "Are we our worst moment?"

Let's dissect the question personally. What was your worst moment?

What would life be like if your identity were rooted in that moment?

What would that say about your future?

Our salvation begins with justification. We are saved from the penalty of sin. Salvation also includes our sanctification, the process and progress of being saved from the power of sin, becoming more and more like Christ each day. Our adoption as children of God is an important and often missed part of our relationship with and identity in Him. Read the following Scripture:

Ephesians 5:1: "Therefore be imitators of God, as beloved children."

1 John 3:1–2: "See what kind of love the Father has given to us, that we should be called children of God; and so we are. The reason why the world does not know us is that it did not know him. Beloved, we are God's children now, and what we will be has not yet appeared; but we know that when he appears we shall be like him, because we shall see him as he is."

Galatians 4:4–7: "But when the fullness of time had come, God sent forth his Son, born of woman, born under the law, to redeem those who were under the law, so that we might receive adoption as sons. And because you are sons, God has sent the Spirit of his Son into our hearts, crying, 'Abba! Father!' So you are no longer a slave, but a son, and if a son, then an heir through God."

I have two biological children and seven children through adoption. I was only able to understand what it means to be a child of God when I could look into the eyes of my adopted children and love them the very same way that I love and care for my biological children. The Gospel is about adoption.

What rights and privileges are granted to those who are adopted into an earthly family? Write down five rights and privileges that we have through our adoption as children of God.

We are not our worst moment, nor are we defined or identified by our greatest achievements. As Christian believers, we are first and foremost God's beloved children, adopted because of the sacrifice of Jesus Christ. How does this biblical truth give you hope? In addition to writing down your answer, jot down a prayer thanking God for adopting you into His Kingdom.

A New Religion:
The Cult of Antiracism

Big Idea

Antiracism is more than a pseduo-religion; it is its own religious movement.

Looking Back

Share one thing that stood out to you most from last week's lesson, video, reading, or discussions.

Primer

The religious overtones of the social justice movement cannot be missed. It has all the trappings of religion. For example, the movement has its own cosmology, its own saints, its own liturgy, and its own law. Some of those aspects are very subtle, which makes for an appealing cause. By now, you recognize this movement is not aligned with Christianity.

In this religion of social justice, and particularly in antiracism, a white person can never do enough to find forgiveness. There's nothing he or she can do to find freedom. Antiracists and the "woke" priesthood are targeting all of us. You might acquiesce to their demands today by apologizing for your "whiteness" or microaggressions or any number of things, but they will continue to demand more and more of you. Your official statements will not be remorseful enough. Your reparations packages will not be big enough. Your diversity initiatives will not be diverse enough. You cannot appease the god of antiracism.

This is why our connection to Jesus Christ is vital: only in Him do we find salvation, redemption, atonement, and reconciliation. He bridges the gap created by sin, which separates us from God. In Jesus, His sacrifice will always be enough.

Ironically, the religion of antiracism is also powerless against racism. It is Christ, and Christ alone, "who has made us both one and has broken down in his flesh the dividing wall of hostility" (Ephesians 2:14). This doesn't mean that black and white Christians won't offend or sin against each other. It also doesn't mean that the sin of racism will not raise its ugly head in the broader culture or even within the Church. What it does mean is that we have an answer. It has been, it is, and it will always be Jesus.

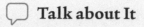 Talk about It

What role does forgiveness play when we are wronged
by another person or a systemic problem?

WATCH THE VIDEO

🎬 Video Teaching Notes

*Watch Video Session 6. Use the outline and space below to jot down notes or
record key ideas.*

- The social justice movement and antiracism are religious in
  their nature.

- This is discouraging because it is a religion that is devoid of
  the Gospel and redemption.

- This "religion" will only crush you and never save you.

- We have the one true religion that leads us to a relationship with the one true and living God.

- If you are drawn toward the religion of social justice and anti-racism, ask yourself why.

💬 Discussion

1. What makes an individual an antiracist?

2. Do you believe Americans are trying to avoid talking about race or trying to control what is being said? Why or why not?

3. In *Fault Lines*, Voddie writes:

> Antiracism offers no salvation—only perpetual penance in an effort to battle an incurable disease. And all of it begins with pouring new meaning into well-known words.

Discuss what it would be like if the Christian religion was not based on the death and resurrection of Jesus Christ and there was no forgiveness of sin, just "perpetual penance."

4. How does antiracism disqualify people from receiving redemption?

5. In *Fault Lines*, Voddie talks about the priesthood of this new religion. Those who qualify for leadership positions only include

> oppressed minorities (people of color, women, LGBTQIA+, non-citizens, the disabled, the obese, the poor, non-Christians, and anyone else with an accepted oppressed status).

How is discrimination at work here?

6. How does the religion of antiracism encourage people to be disingenuous or biased?

7. Give examples of progress you have seen to help minimize racial discrimination over the last twenty years.

8. What is the hope found in the Gospel message?

Wrap-Up and Closing Prayer

Today we learned that the movement of antiracism is a religion marked by destructive heresies intended to crush, rather than reconcile.

You can pray the following prayer to close this session, or say one your way:

> God, thank You for the truth of the Gospel message and that through the death and resurrection of Your Son I have freedom and life everlasting. Give me the strength, courage, and wisdom to act as Your image-bearer on Earth. Bring significance to whatever I may accomplish on this earth. In Christ's name I pray, amen.

SESSION 6

Between Sessions

DAY 1

In *Fault Lines*, Voddie introduces the concept of "Ethnic Gnosticism," a term he coined several years ago. Gnosticism is derived from the Greek word *gnosis* (knowledge) and is based on the idea that truth can be accessed through special, mystical knowledge. Ethnic Gnosticism is the dangerous and growing idea that people have special knowledge based solely on their ethnicity. This is a hallmark of both Critical Race Theory and its predecessor, Critical Theory. While *Fault Lines* covers the idea of Ethnic Gnosticism in detail, including its three basic manifestations, it's worth mentioning in this session.

Ethnic Gnosticism essentially says that because of a person's particular ethnicity, he or she will have special knowledge of oppression without needing evidence or facts to support his or her "truth." Additionally, Ethnic Gnosticism affords the right to label individuals as racists not because of proof or evidence, but because of their ethnicity (in this case, their whiteness).

Read Jeremiah 17:9: "The heart is deceitful above all things, and desperately sick; who can understand it?"

Why does the Bible define our hearts as wicked?

How can we make sure we engage with others not by what our "heart" tells us, but by what God says?

One of the ways Ethnic Gnosticism negatively impacts humankind is by compromising genuine relationships. If one person assumes he or she can read another person's heart, that relationship is imbalanced, and that assumption will hinder true intimacy and growth.

Read 1 Corinthians 13:1-8:

> If I speak in the tongues of men and of angels, but have not love, I am a noisy gong or a clanging cymbal. And if I have prophetic powers, and understand all mysteries and all knowledge, and if I have all faith, so as to remove

mountains, but have not love, I am nothing. If I give away all I have, and if I deliver up my body to be burned, but have not love, I gain nothing.

Love is patient and kind; love does not envy or boast; it is not arrogant or rude. It does not insist on its own way; it is not irritable or resentful; it does not rejoice at wrong-doing, but rejoices with the truth. Love bears all things, believes all things, hopes all things, endures all things.

Love never ends. As for prophecies, they will pass away; as for tongues, they will cease; as for knowledge, it will pass away.

How does the above Scripture teach us how to love others the way God loves us?

How is this biblical and God-centered love antithetical to Ethnic Gnosticism?

DAY 2

The religion of antiracism includes the idea of works-based right-eousness, yet according to the Gospel, Christ has atoned for our sins. Read Ephesians 4:31–32:

> Let all bitterness and wrath and anger and clamor and slander be put away from you, along with all malice. Be kind to one another, tenderhearted, forgiving one another, as God in Christ forgave you.

Why does God command us to forgive one another?

How does forgiveness in Christ offer freedom as compared to con-stantly having to apologize and live in guilt for having a certain skin color, as in the religion of antiracism?

How can unforgiveness lead to bitterness?

Read the following Scriptures:

Psalm 86:5: "For you, O Lord, are good and forgiving, abounding in steadfast love to all who call upon you."

Psalm 103:12: "As far as the east is from the west, so far does he remove our transgressions from us."

Micah 7:18: "Who is a God like you, pardoning iniquity and passing over transgression for the remnant of his inheritance? He does not retain his anger forever, because he delights in steadfast love."

Ephesians 1:7-8: "In Him we have redemption through His blood, the forgiveness of sins, according to the riches of His grace which He made to abound toward us in all wisdom and prudence."

1 John 1:9: "If we confess our sins, he is faithful and just to forgive us our sins and to cleanse us from all unrighteousness."

Write down three characteristics of the forgiving nature of God.

If we refuse to forgive, we step into dangerous waters. First, refusing to forgive is to put ourselves in the place of God, as though vengeance were our prerogative, not His. Second, unforgiveness says God's wrath is insufficient. Finally, refusing to forgive is the highest form of arrogance. Here we stand forgiven; yet we act as though the sins of others are too significant to forgive while simultaneously believing that ours are not significant enough to matter.

In the end, it is forgiveness that will heal our wounds.

Endnotes

1. *Oxford English Dictionary*, s.v. "social justice."
2. Teri Dugan, "A Case for the Bible 101: How Does Archeological Evidence Support the Readability of the Old Testament?" *True Faith and Reason*, May 18, 2018, https://truthfaithandreason.com/a-case-for-the-bible-101-how-does-archeological-evidence-support-the-reliability-of-the-old-testament/.
3. David J. Johnson et al., "Officer Characteristics and Racial Disparities in Fatal Officer-Involved Shootings," *Proceedings of the National Academy of Sciences* 116, no. 32 (August 6, 2019): 15877–15882, first published on July 22, 2019, https://doi.org/10.1073/pnas.1903856116. Their study was attacked immediately as racist. One researcher was demoted from his position at Michigan State University for citing it. Eventually, the authors retracted the study, though it was peer-reviewed and they still stand behind their findings. Moreover, the findings mirror those of a similar study in 2015.
4. "Fatal Force," *Washington Post*, updated May 24, 2022, https://www.washingtonpost.com/graphics/investigations/police-shootings-database/.
5. Örjan Falk et al., "The 1% of the Population Accountable for 63% of All Violent Crime Convictions," *Social Psychiatry and Psychiatric Epidemiology* 49, no. 4 (April 2014): 559–71. John MacArthur, "What Is Biblical Discernment? Why Is It Important?," Christianity.com, January 12, 2021, https://www.christianity.com/theology/what-is-biblical-discernment-and-why-is-it-important-11532182.html.
6. Richard Delgado, *Critical Race Theory*, 3rd ed., (New York: New York University Press), 8, Kindle edition.
7. Ibid., 9.
8. Ibid.
9. Ibid., 10–11.
10. "What Is Critical Race Theory?" UCLA School of Public Affairs, https://spacrs.wordpress.com/what-is-critical-race-theory/#_ftn1.
11. "Turning the Corner on Father Absence in Black America: A Statement from the Morehouse Conference on African American Fathers," Morehouse Research Institute & Institute for American Values, Morehouse College, Fall 1998; Voddie Baucham Jr., *Fault Lines: The Social Justice Movement and Evangelicalism's Looming Catastrophe* (Washington, D.C.: Salem Books, 2021), 176, Kindle edition.
12. "Text of Obama's Fatherhood Speech," Politico, June 15, 2008, https://www.politico.com/story/2008/06/text-of-obamas-fatherhood-speech-011094.
13. The Editors of Encyclopedia Britannica, "The Three-Fifths Compromise," *Encyclopedia Britannica*, https://www.britannica.com/topic/three-fifths-compromise.
14. Jemar Tisby, *The Color of Compromise* (Grand Rapids, Michigan: Zondervan, 2019), 59, Kindle edition. Interestingly, Tisby discusses the relevant issues and includes the relevant evidence, but still draws an inconsistent conclusion.
15. Heather Griffiths et al., *Introduction to Sociology 2e* (Houston, Texas: OpenStax, 2015).
16. Helen Pluckrose and James Lindsay, *Cynical Theories* (Durham, North Carolina: Pitchstone Publishing, 2020), Kindle edition.